A PURE BEAD

❦

Allegra Wong

A PURE BEAD

Allegra Wong

— Del Sol Press • Washington D. C.—

CONTENTS

CONTENTS, CONTINUED

To my son, Emerson

Again, somehow, one saw life, a pure bead.
—Virginia Woolf, "The Death of the Moth"

I

THE LONELY DOLLS

They thought we were cloth
with painted faces and yarn braids.
Up close though, after they dragged us
away from the rim where he had taken us,
they could see our faces were powdered, rouged.
They could see our skin.

When they straitjacketed him and walked him
down the front steps of our cottage,
we broke free, hand in hand.

House wrens bubbled. Wood thrushes fluted.
Yellow and orange butterflies ringed
around gravestones growing along the roadside.
Bees hummed over black-eyed Susans.

We entered the forest and listened to the tick
of an elm with a glass heart in its trunk.
In the moonlight on the lane
a little pink house caught us in his arms,
hugged us. He twirled, reached inside himself
through one of his windows, took out three birds.

"Let's wear these," he said.
For her, the indigo bunting.
For me, the red-winged blackbird.
"That leaves the goldfinch in spring,"
said the little pink house, "for me."

Birds pinned in our hair, we wandered
among pines drinking jasmine from thin china cups,
oaks playing cello.

We tired.
Nettles closed over our path.
Eels from the swamp curled around us, snaked us
to the elm. Our birds flew up into its bonnet fretwork.
The little pink house offered himself as firewood.

BECOMING

Were you the one who looked after me
that night in the woods?
I was not yet fully formed—half wing
half whistle—and I flew from bough
to bough of the tallest evergreens.

The blood in your veins was loud
like breezes in white pines.
My heartbeat, a colt galloping
twice as fast as your pulse.
The sigh of the placenta, the promise
of bougainvillea and pink ginger

segueing into your voice,
and the slender pony-tailed altar boy
who would jump from the bell tower of Catedral de San Juan.
Terrorists who would walk me to San Cristóbal, gun me.
A mortician who would wrap my head in gauze.

SUBTERRANEANS

Beneath the Mass Ave Bridge, he joins them in lantern light,
transsexuals handing around rations from
the Pine Street Shelter, mumbling to him
about who was found dead at dawn beneath the lavender-wing
vine. He's their auntie, come to pilot them
in the river wind, half-men who cruise the esplanade
at midnight, seeking men to spread their seed—fluttering,
getting off where they are.

GIFT-GIVING

Beauty-In-Heels sits in the park, translates *Ulysses*
into the American drag queen idiom.
In short-shorts, he tans on the bench, then stands,
peers into boughs and nests. Stretches
to see into rooms of taut men and their crewcut mates.
Obituaries slow.
Beauty-In-Heels tires of holding hands with himself.
He smells circuit parties, hears the siren of Barebackjack.com.
Feeling good in Powerhouse back room, he pill pops for therapy.

Valentine lounges on the park bench.
He smokes, drinks wine, slicks back his hair
and gives another voice to Joyce Calypso lines.
Valentine stands, heavy-girthed,
his black pants crease. His hand bleeds at one joint.
Herpes tendril from his left hip to his heart.
Monogamous, now, he walks
past a new block of saplings.

Ishmael always sits on the park bench, reads Joyce.
His black pants gray, hands brown.
Black hollyhock blooms on his cheeks and arms.
His hair thins. He loses weight. Sheer now,
he cannot hold his book. His space
on the bench is moist. Oaks leaf, shade.

Gift-giving: 1. when HIV-positive people (who know they are positive) have un-
protected sex with other people and don't tell these others they are positive.
2. being HIV-positive and having unprotected sex with HIV-negative people who *want*
to become HIV-positive. By becoming positive, the HIV-negative people feel they no longer
have to worry about becoming positive. Others feel that by becoming HIV-positive they
join an *in* group, and finally they belong. Some HIV-negative people (a subculture of
gay men mostly) actively seek gift-giving, through personal ads, from HIV-positive people.

YOU KNOW ME, I'M IN EVERY DOWNTOWN

Glossy as licorice, tatted with snow,
fire escapes zigzag brick walk-ups,
merchants unshutter their shops. Charlene Choi's
Such A Better Day tinkles from a tea garden.

Along the street, a gathering of queens
sing, a cappella, Richard Lam's *Love You More*,
some dark meat, some aunties, some angels
among them. I hear my choice—
the falsetto with goldened hair
and waxed brows. I follow him

to his room, stand at his window and watch
older men practice "Grasping the Bird's Tail"
in Mulberry Bend Park. I turn to him.
He's a whole man who asks to be taken.
I pull down his pants.
He's already a little hard.

Back on the street, I choose a queen,
the one that catches my eye,
the alto I slightly know, an auntie
with slender hips, similar, similar
to me, I mean, a pre-op transgender.

Up in his room, he strips as I close the door.
His bed against the window overlooks
green and yellow roof tops, chimney pots,
an occasional line of laundry. Beyond,
the Manhattan Bridge soars. East River's dusky blue.

I feel so lost in the city, shacked up
with a stranger. But wide-seeing.
Once I've taken off my clothes, I'm home.
I kiss his silky thighs—*let me make you happy*
these moments you are mine.

LUNCH WITHOUT FRANK

There are some among us who are righteous men.
There are many among us who do nothing but evil.
We must strike off the heads of the unbelievers, then,
and strike off all of their fingertips.
       —from the Old Testament and the Qur'an

He picks at a sore on his left thumb.
His fingernails are still buffed, as they were in life.
Have some drag fun, babe, he says, while Seth's away.
Silk your hair, pull on a short skirt, dark stockings,
take Seth's Beamer for a spin on the Pike,
drive up alongside truckers. See what happens.

He lights a Marlboro.
Or walk the mall. Look in the windows,
basket shop the mannequins. After a while,
you'll see a hot pants has been watching you.
He draws on his cigarette.

   (He still smells the four they burned in North Chinatown,
   the corpses of three strung up on the Manhattan Bridge.
   A chunk of flesh sawn off the backside of the fourth,
   tied to a brick and thrown over an electric line.)

I stir sugar into my coffee,
smell his aftershave, his whiskey.
"I miss you."
I'm your first boyfriend, for Christ's sake.
The old sugar daddy.
But his eyes are moist.
Yeah, your first lover…

(Six veiled men dressed in black circle him, use machetes.)

"I need you. Now, afternoons."
You don't need me to make you happy,
go around the world on you.
Maybe Seth doesn't do that, but Seth gets in deep, doesn't he?

(He screams as the first slits his throat.
His captors intone, "Christ died for your sake."
Minutes later, one of the captors holds up his severed head.)

Here you sit while Seth's hitting the tea rooms,
having anonymous sex in public places…
He laughs, then taps his cigarette ash into his left hand.
Isn't that how you two broncos met?

I want him to rock me against his chest.
Brush my hair. Suggest martinis and bed.

(His body is discovered at 7:30 p.m. local time.
His head has been left outside the Mott Street Baptist Church.)

Don't worry, babe. There's something about buggering deep
that'll keep a man coming home to you.
Maybe for a lifetime.

I ache to touch him.
Put an end to dreams of Baptists who break in
through the skylight, rope-haul me to the roof,
believe I'm saved, made whole
at their moment of beheading me.

COME OUT WITH US!

Cherry-lipped, champagne-haired crones walk
damp Broadway. They rub up against shops,
their breaths steaming windows of chevron
and squab, Nicaraguan cigars.
Their leather jackets smolder.
Their chins sprout billy goat hairs.

Arms around one another,
they're going steady.
Eleanor, Ruth, Constance—
names of unrequited loves tumble from their lips
as they gather the words of the young
falling around them like bird eyes:

Don't close up on me.
Don't ever lie to me.
Never protect yourself with me.

II

WHERE I COME FROM

A bare bulb hangs in my South Boston kitchen,
what I stare at Sunday evenings
during those years of junior high, during
Clarence's string of questions
after my father's leaving.

Visiting hours over, the weekly
child support check safe in my mother's bed
—after each question from Clarence, her lover,
a slap in the face—
Did you tell your daddy I touch you?
Did you tell him where and how?

Without or with my head wrapped
in a scarf, I can do whatever I please
with this barfly in The Eliot.
He's bought my confessions of taboo sex.

MY MOTHER'S LOVER, MICK

Sharpens a paring knife on diamond
hone at an angle of 19 degrees,
points to my cold fried fish lunch.

Wielding the paring knife, he lunges at me.

Nights I watch by lampglow.
Bedroom door slightly ajar, I see Mother
stride her lover. Bed sheet slides away.
With one hand, he finger fucks Mother, with the other,
rubs his cock. Mother's ass, two white altar lilies.
Her pubic thatch, long, coarse—like llama hair.
Licking, kissing, sucking his lips,
my child-sized mother seems to tear and eat
her lover's flesh.

When Mother leaves for work, Mick bathes,
calls for me to wash his back.
I soap him with Lux.

Unable to make him come by lathering his cock,
I crouch by the toilet, pee my pants.
Mother's lover pees on me.

He naps, towel-wrapped, atop Mother's bed.

I wait on the front porch for Mother.
Touch her sweater's pearly buttons.

Mother closes the plastic curtains, insists I tub soak.
Mick joins us, leans down on us, our three faces
nearly touching at tubside. He has gifts. For me,

a new drawstring leather marble bag; for Mother, perfume—
Evening in Paris silver-scripted on the bottle's dark blue face.

One afternoon, my mother's lover
takes his belt to me, strikes until my nose bleeds,
mashes the buckle in my mouth.

He naps, towel-wrapped, atop Mother's bed.

With my X-acto blade, razored
at an angle of 11 degrees, I nick him.
He wakes.

That night Mother takes me to her room, tells
of her dead grandmother, Margaret, tied to a board.
Margaret bathed, night-gowned by her daughter-in-law
while the undertaker prepared her casket for parlor display.

"I was four years old, running through downstairs rooms
looking for my mother. Someone pointed
to a closed door. I rushed in, saw Margaret
strapped to a board straight up against the wall."

Mother pauses.
"Does that story bother you?"
"No," I say.
"Means you're like me then. Because my telling it
bothered Mick tonight. He's had to pack and leave."

INT. STANDARD ARTIST'S STUDIO

(A woman is pacing the room, paying little attention to the artist
at his easel.)

Take off your clothes.
Let me get the feel of you
on canvas. I need to start
some studies for the portrait
I want to do of you.

(She slips out of her blouse and dungarees, and sits on the arm
of the couch. He looks at her as he sketches.)

I wouldn't mind knowing a youth
I could watch just like the writer does
in the video I've been renting. Except
I'd want to see the boy's cock erect.
I'd want to hold it. Draw energy from it.
Wouldn't want to do anything though.

(She flexes her toes.)

I visited a masseur.
He touched; I could touch him back.
I felt safe.

(She yawns and looks toward the clock.)

He painted, too. Had a show—*Animal Under Observation.*
Isolation. Relationship. Monster Love.
Skulls—Studies of Individuals.

(She chews bubble gum.)

The redhead in Queens led me
to her room, took off my clothes.
I couldn't do anything.
I was small, soft.
She was picking up quick money sketching
some clubs—chubs, pseudo-necrophiliacs,
bondage, toilet training, back alley Special K 'rapes'.

Stop moving, please!

Beth liked poetry about cruelty.
After a plague, after cruelty,
only death or purification is left.
Cruelty's a primitive ceremonial experience.
Cruelty's a call for communion.

(He cuts his thumb, gets the right color of red on the canvas.)

Andy, beefcake—I did it with him
by the old railroad where the cattle are brought in.
You'd have to cover your nose sometimes.
You'd walk through what had fallen off—
feet, tails, heads, skins, entrails, it's all about…

Stop moving, please!

(It's snowing outside.
He puts on his overcoat, opens the windows.
Lowers the heat—he wants her pale.)

...stunning—cattle are dismembered
and hogs scalded while still conscious.

It wasn't just Hieronymous Bosch—
his nightmares, his spectres. His belief
in a world corrupted by man that influenced me.
I was also studying 'meat'.

Yesterday ran ads again in *Poppy*.
Instead of the usual foul-mouthed whores,
I found you.

(He locks the door and pockets the key.)

I think that in your arms, everything
would be there, for it begins
with finding someone to whom I can talk.

BOSTON MORNING, 340 BEACON STREET

A nude stands back from the window
towel in hand. Outside, brownstones
hide their rooms behind green shades.
A ray of sun catches the gold
on the walls. It streaks her limbs, her breasts,

her red hair. She remembers the sea at Dorado,
how she waited in her lover's doorway,
barefoot in a blue dress
with all the buttons undone—
breast, belly, thighs.

How he sprinted up the path, dripping
from his swim.
"Looking for me?"

She remembers cooling off on the patio,
watching the cottage yard across the path,
a man in a red shirt, a woman in a blue blouse,
swinging in a hammock.
How they talked of life after death,
listened to—was it Mahler?

"No," she thought. "For love."

PAST BROWNSTONES WITH WHITE ROOFTOPS

Just home from welding, just in from the snowy street,
I'd kiss your belly and thighs,
but I was never a john for thirty dollars.

Your back so pale. Pulling on
your salmon swimsuit in our small room.

How quickly you're trapped again,
stealing from the shops in fair weather,
cutting at your long hair when there were clouds,
chopping apart your doll because you were wondering
what made bad blood as you coughed in your sleep.

You, waiting for me undressed,
huddled under the patchwork quilt you grew up with;
you, with empty suitcases strapped to hands, filling space,
leaving the stairwells of this city—
you are porcelain.

LANDSDOWNE STREET BAR

In a red silk sheath, she passes from man to man.
Hands press on her hips. Curve of calves.
Waist. One man asks for a dance. Another a kiss.

She is surrounded by men, men who make soft crying sounds
as they run their fingers along her throat, inside her
wrists, thighs. Men who nuzzle her breasts, brush

her tight ass. One pleads for pussy.
"Let me smell it, like an animal. No one will see."
He licks her, gently.

She glides into the dark, a figure in flames,
smelling of wind and salt.

III

LITTLE MOTHER

When I saw her, I was building a sand castle
on the beach with my son.

She walked toward us, her arms filled with mangoes.
She was lightly embalmed and in a dark blue dress.
I put her down to rest in a cool room
at the back of our screenless cottage. It was late morning.

In the kitchen, I washed and peeled the mangoes,
sliced some, and my son and I placed their peach-sweet flesh
on our tongues. I heard her stir.
I mashed some left slices, pressed juice from others,

put the mash onto a saucer with a small spoon.
I sat on the floor beside her in the now dusky room,
lighted a lamp, and fed her the pulp
then resealed her lips with the juice.
Straightened her hands,
the white collar of her dress.

She slipped back into her death.

And while my young son built as the sun set
I was happy in the tropical evening light,
happier than I could ever be
in similar light in northern woods, my source.

Because she needed to learn she was in death,
to stop twisting her hands, to stop becoming thin,
I tucked her in a coffin, a birch.
I was young. I could carry it—
it was light and soft like a quilt.

She smelled of gardenias from the mortuary.
I lifted her in my arms, walked out of the cottage,
my son skipped ahead, pointed the way to her tomb.

In the dusk of the tomb I found I had become old
and little mother in the box was stiff.

See the black marks along her temples,
the green along her throat and ears?

Was I one of those daughters
who died from missing their mothers?

HIXVILLE, MASSACHUSETTS

Her longing for smell brought her back
to Hixville. *North & South, Questions of Travel.*
She talks of her three-day trip to Key West, how
standing at the gate of Bishop's White Street,
she believed she could identify origins
by journeying far from her territory.

She understands she is dead.

"Did anyone see FDR arrive by limousine
for his postmaster's burial? Did anyone
see me at age seventeen waiting for Eleanor
in the Civil War heroes' circle?"

Mother asks me to stroke her shoulders, wet
her lips with strawberries and grapes.
Her vault is sealed with epoxy.
Her casket is locked, her mouth sewn shut.

"Talk to me so the darkness will lift."

Near her grave, the boughs
break over infant headstones.
The stone angel is blue in the cold.
Snowflakes drop through her hand
shaped to carry a pansy bouquet.

FALL RIVER, 1956

After my sister died, I crouched in the kitchen,
pared snow apples for my doll, asleep on a rug beside me.
Grandmother, by evening windows,
peeled lamb kidneys for English pie.

A mother was not present,
neither in the sewing room or in the pantry where
the black-handled bread knife waited to slice warm loaves,
and my grandmother probed,
with the bone-handled fork, the cooking kidneys.

And Great-grandmother's pestle, black iron
whorls around an iron handle—whorls
silvering along their edges—lay in a wooden bowl.

And these are your mother's,
my grandmother murmured
as she watered heliotrope seedlings
growing in cheeseboxes on the windowsills.

No one knows our cupboards were filled
with English soaps
and not just mourning.
Cakes of lavender and rose, each tissue-wrapped,
were tucked in a box
with a London street scene on its cover.
I would hold a cake of soap
and say it nestled in my palm
the way a pet warbler might,
the way your palm nestled in your sister's, remember?

The London street was not a place
we hoped someday to visit.
But somehow one of the cottages, its window curtains drawn wide,
hinted my sister,
dressed in her homemade corduroys, lived inside.

YOU WANT TO WALK DOWN THE LANE

With your mother who has letters to mail
to her first-born. The two of you
wave good-bye to your doll at the window,
journey past the nunnery, the orphans home,
the iron gates of Oak Grove Cemetery.

You want to walk past snowballs and wisteria
jostling. Moonlight whitens gravel, invites you
to step on crisscrossing branch shadows.
You want to walk down the lane
but you don't
because the state hospital, nearly hidden,
grows. You visited there once.
Women clasped dolls to their breasts,
men waved from locked rooms. You visited there once.
The community room, upon your arrival,
promised permission to speak
whenever you were ready. It was hard to leave,
but you shouldn't have been playing still with your doll.

It was hard to leave, but you did.
Women kissed you to stay.
Men pressed their erections against your hips.
Nin erotica volumes subsisted on your bookshelf,
and when you approached, opened them,
skimmed lines, they fluttered, startled.
One whimpered, one whispered to others.
You listened.

It was the moonlight slanting through windows,
on your way to the community room,
that called you out, made you believe

you saw your mother hurrying
along the Fall River streets
with her handful of night letters,
and you, a girl with thick black braids,
waving good-bye to your doll.

THE LAST PRIVATE OPINION

I miss hands, please touch me,
the nickel revolver whispers when I find it
at the back of Mother's desk drawer.
It guides my fingertips, suggests
I trace its silhouette.
I pull back.
I'll learn to love its shiny barrel, black handle
with a waffle weave, its absence
of a safety catch, its fit
in my trousers pocket.
Bullets are easy to buy on the Internet.

Grandfather bought the double action 32 cal. rim fire,
the morning after the hold-up in his corner grocery.
In its original U.S. Revolver Co. black box,
Grandmother shoved it, deep into her pocketbook
the evening she smelled another woman's
moistness in my grandfather's hair.
Mother tucked the revolver in the holster
of my dead sister's Annie Oakley outfit,
third drawer down in her bird's-eye maple chest.

The revolver saved the grocery
and my grandmother's marriage,
but my sister died two years after I was born.

Father drank whiskey evenings,
and when Mother locked him out,
nickel flashed in her hands at the storm door.

On the front steps of the Hixville house
where she moved with George, my stepfather,
Mother practiced shooting the revolver.
I'd wonder, coming home from school, had a hunter
come too close, swinging a bouquet of dead pheasant?

Or did Mother still believe someone—my dead sister,
my dead grandparents—entered the house,
watched while she napped afternoons.

Or had Father, needing money, burgled?

After Father's breakdown, Mother phoned him
each day, drove to his rooming house
when he didn't answer. Sometimes he was napping
or said he missed his pal, my sister.
Mother swore she always smelled gas.

When I take the revolver home to Boston,
after Mother dies, I lift it
from its box tearing at the corners.
Pop in the bullets,
slide the barrel into the frame.
Walk out to the Charles River esplanade
at dawn. Pull back the trigger.
The revolver smokes a bit.

Sometimes I think Mother tucked the revolver
in the holster of the Annie Oakley outfit

not for the protection of my sister in eternity,
not so my sister could carry a real gun in the afterlife.
And not to protect me.
But as an offering to Father
stalking her room, missing his pal, Father,
not there to wound Mother,
but to kill himself.

HIXVILLE, 1999

My mother no longer sits in her chair with the Spanish feet,
flannel robe wrapping her thin shoulders, puffy belly,
her bald head growing first down.

Seasons after her death, she rustles,
sounds like she's in taffeta, the '60s blue
she wore evenings to the Colonial Theater, her talks
backstage with Le Gallienne and Gielgud.
The blue she wore afternoons when she waved to me
as she stood on the bridge in the Boston Public Garden
and I sailed close in a boat shaped like a swan.

She'd wear white cotton gloves.
I'd call up to her, *hello, hello.*
She'd call back, *farewell, farewell.* We'd laugh.
She'd lean over the railing, wave again, and blow me a kiss.
My swan would slide beneath the bridge.

Today she walks her rooms, reciting her Fall River years—
shopping McWhirr's for a winter coat,
having her hair waved at Janet's Salon.
Buying sun suits and sunbonnets, toy boats shaped like swans
for her babies, and decades later, for mine.
Re-reading *To the Lighthouse, The Voyage Out.*

When I have learned how to die, she says, *I will know how to belong.*

I call to my mother, ask her to stay. She rustles, slides back
the bolt on the front door, hurries out.
Her Cinderella heels click along the brick walk.
At the rise in the driveway, she turns and blows me a kiss,
mistaking the rise for a bridge,
my call for the hello of a child sailing past in a swan.

GRASP

Gladioli staked and incarnadine
shadowed by wrought iron,
the smell of rain.

Inside, you hook your two silver canes
on the back of her chair. Hunched over
the chrome table, you sit with her again.

You've ordered ragout.
While you wait, you tear pita
into rectangles, squares, dip some into roe.

You push your chair close,
feed her morsels.

One rainy night, when you were seventeen,
you got chills fishing at Fresh Pond,
but packed for camp the next morning.
There you roomed with a boy who died
from polio later that summer.

"It was because of the pitch-black pond
and night air…" you correct her,
"and not the boy with whom I roomed."

You fumble for her fingers, wince
as you identify in her thumb
her opposing muscle,
the grasp which separates her
from chimpanzees.

THE OTHER SIDE

The tall thin woman with a baby in her arms
and the short man in a trench coat are walking her garden,
peering at the robin nest in the fallen apple tree.
They step on her pansies and four o'clocks.

She runs into the attic.
A Moses basket, woven from oriole nests,
hangs from the ladder leading to the skylight.
Hornets buzz in the hood.
Let us in. We need to warm a bottle for the baby,
the woman calls from the garden.
We left the grave at dawn today.
She crouches beneath the rack of old maternity clothes.
A bottle for the baby.

Her husband pulls into the driveway, lets them in.
She burrows into a bundle of lambswool,
takes out her dead newborn's sacque, the pink brushed cotton.
She thinks she hears her husband in the kitchen filling a pan with water
to warm the baby's bottle.
Clasping the brushed cotton sacque to her,

she climbs the ladder and opens the skylight. She steps out
into a forest, pine boughs laden with nests
of baby boys and baby girls.
Some nests are lined with lengths of horse mane,
some with plant down and spider webs.
Each nest is collared with new snow.

NEAR ELLENSBURG

In astral lamp light, Jotul-warm,
she reads of houses emptied after death,
impressions of life beyond her wrists,
of middle-aged children carrying out
candelabra, Bristol vases, paintings
their parents purchased together.

She listens to the Jotul green wood
fire and him showering, smells coffee brewing,
and she mistakes Puget Sound, outside the window,
for pink sky breaking the paper-white and gray.

She and he, companions now,
have known Ballard winter nights
sharing Richard Hugo and James Welch passages.
Summer afternoons stopping
in Hoh River Valley
to examine licorice ferns crowning cedars
at the shore, they mistake the calls of cormorants
and petrels nesting in the sea stacks
for the voices of sea lions.

Near Ellensburg, in a small pasture cemetery,
she mistakes a lamb's cry for a human mother's
over her dead child. The solitary opening,
permits her—and him—to glimpse her mother busy
even in death bathing her sister.

Remembrances too big to hold in their arms
like vases or paintings, remembrances like
chrysanthemums spilling along a chipped brick path
when the rampant hollyhocks and roses

shrouded the picket fence. She would run
past her dead sister's toy desk
to a hollow beneath the wisteria
in the rank back garden
and listen to neighbor children buy chocolate
from the singing sidewalk candy man,
tinkling bells sewn to his shirt.

Remembrances so big, that they caress,
suggest how long it takes to love, how long
it takes to stop touching, stop wanting to touch.

AFTER MY MOTHER DIES, I SIT IN HER HIXVILLE HOUSE

While she, pink-jumpered, walks coops,
reaches in nests, fills baskets with brown eggs,
heads out to Copicut in her '41 Studebaker.

She passes Dell's potato fields in North Westport
eager for home and her reading—
L'Allegro and *Il Penseroso*—
but Dell, watching her drive past, guides her

to his house, asks her to dance. Barefoot, she dances
over the orange and ocher tiles of his garden.
Bridal wreath matures along the brick walls
as his hands lead her away, through woods

to this house. I am forty-two years old.
My mother, twenty-seven, is dancing with Dell.
She looks over at me, but says nothing, knowing
I will share in her sorrow.

IV

WHAT YOU THINK LOVE WOULD BE LIKE

Leopold Bloom crossing Eccles Street, inventing as he walks
the island of Dublin, following a trail of smells
from his kitchen's hot coals, the warmbubbled milk
for his cat, and the tea he is making for Molly,
upstairs lying in bed, singing love songs, weaving lies
about the stamina of her twenty-five suitors.

Molly knitting, or remembering knitting,
the little woolen jacket for baby Rudy to wear in his grave,
to O'Rourke's, and its whiffs of ginger, teadust, and biscuitmush.

The National School windows open for fresh air.

Bloom daydreaming of an east with carpets and stalls
and a plum moon, the color of Molly's garters.
Stocking his dream of the east with melon fields,
Molly's ass—cool, waxen fruit—which he kisses each night,
"skin so delicate white like wax"—
or the porcelains containing her perfumes.

(The word 'porcelain' coming from the Latin
for the genitals of a female pig.
Porcelain, silky like a vagina.
Civet, honey from the genitals of the Ethiopian cat;
musk, red jelly from the lower guts of East Asian deer—
he'd know her perfume in a thousand—
a silky mouth, a yes, holding the secretions of cats and deer.)

Or a street in lower Manhattan, one that blends
the shafts of Wall, silk markets of Canal,
rug merchants of lower Broadway, shine of the Chrysler spire,
the square where feral cats nurse their torn pads,

the rubbled plaza where you lean to watch the light
first on the Woolworth Building,
then on mangled steel columns and girders, the charred finches.

ROSE ON ROSE

He thinks about the three minutes he was breathing in rosewater.
Closing his lids to the nectar.

Then he joins Poldy in their favorite booth in the back of Rosie's.
Poldy has ordered them chips and fish, himself another beer.

    In ancient Rome, says Stephen, adjusting his tie,
    rose water bubbled through the emperor's fountain,
    surged in the public baths.

'Her roses'—
what my Molly calls her bleeding, says Poldy,
as he trims a callus on his thumb with his pocketknife.

    Men and women wore rose perfume.
    Pillows were stuffed with rose petals,
    and rose pudding was a favorite dessert.

The stale smell of her full red lips, drinking,
says Poldy between swigs of beer.
Their Chianti sweetness. Gluey.
Her soiled 'roses' underpants.

    Roman spas were patterned after Egyptian baths, and the walls,
    whenever possible, were of rosewood.
    Stephen lights a cigarette, takes a first sip of beer.

Poldy accepts the trembling rosy gland, the kidney,
from the barmaid. He squeezes it, orders it sauteed, hands it back.
"My scrotum, my soft penis. Molly's full red lips."

After bathing, the Egyptians soaked their clothes
in rose perfume baths.
Their washed bodies underwent aromatherapy.
Stephen draws on his cigarette, examines his neatly trimmed nails.

Poldy calls it toothsome pliant meat,
this flesh dead like those interred in Roman graveyards.
He chews tobacco, then spits it into the paper coffee cup
he carries with him.

The Egyptians applied this technique and process
of rose water baths and aromatherapy to themselves
after noticing how successful
a mummifying technique it was for their dead.

This rosy gland cooled
until I choose to purchase it.
Poldy licks chip crumbs from between his fingers.

During orgies, says Stephen, Romans layered the floors with roses.
Couples and groups loved in them.
He places his cigarette on the ashtray edge, lifts a forkful of fish to his lips.

Poldy reaches for the barmaid's blotchy and sausagepink fingers,
then takes the plate of kidney from her chapped red hands.
Cuts away the burnt flesh to the moist and tender rosiness.

A rosary—165 dried rolled-up roses,
Stephen daubs at his mouth with his napkin,
for a rose is the symbol of the Virgin Mary.

My Molly's roses, a bath that is bloodwarm and rose red.
Poldy sops up the kidney gravy with his bread,
eats the kidney, its changed blood and flesh.

WHEN AN ENGINEER NEEDS A WOMAN

He seats her at his work station,
points to an asterisk on the screen.
"I'm not like the other engineers. I do
my artificial intelligence at the embryonic level.
I've begun adding temporary memory to ARTIE,
my animat, so he can take action
based on an intention.
Now I want to develop ARTIE as a machine."

He hands her a paper filled with equations.
"ARTIE's food," he says, "for his hunger."
She shrugs. "Hunger?"
"Call it what you like: sex, food, play."
"What do you call it?"
"Fucking. When I make ARTIE into a machine,
he's going to fuck, literally. And ARTIE will know
that eros is laughing, caressing, babbling."
"Then you'll need a robot he can love."

He checks his watch. Walks to the window.
Points across the narrow courtyard.
"Third window up, second from right."
The leg and hand of a robot lie on a work table.
A man sits back, holds a robot in his hands.
A woman leans close holding another, lifts
it rhythmically over his.
"You watch them regularly?"

He nods. "Some days it's a different
assistant, some days a different boss."
"Why aren't you there?"
"ARTIE's not ready yet."

* In a computer simulation that attempts to capture interesting though perhaps very simplified aspects of an animal's behavior, but including a degree of adaptation to its environment, and displays a representation of the simulated animal, the resulting artificial creature is called an animat.

WHEN A WOMAN WANTS A ROBOT

I.

She dresses in a slim-fitting black skirt and fuchsia summer sweater,
crosses Technology Square, enters Salvatore's coffee shop,
and scans the back wall.
She walks past chipped Formica tables,
singles and couples talking,
stops where a man in his fifties, in a tweed jacket,
sits alone reading *The Robot's Path.*

With her fingertips, she touches his shoulder.
He tosses aside his book and stands. "You
didn't tell me you're pretty! Take that chair.
The light won't be in your eyes."

Coming here was a mistake, she thinks. I'm so nervous.

He holds the chair for her. "Sit.
Cappuccino? Latte?"

II.

They meet again at Salvatore's,
sit closer to each other on the same side of the table.
"When we talked on the phone that first time, I liked
you sight unseen," she says. "I've been wanting a lover."
She strokes his wrist.

"My first ad," he replies. "Lucky me."

She lets him take her hand. "You're
going to like me as a friend, too," he says.
"Am I? Your ad sounded so depraved: *Robot Seeking Erotic Ways.*"
"Why didn't that scare you off?"
"I've been wanting a lover."

STILL LIFE

Not a bowl of oranges, grapes, with pomegranate,
but the man I love, dressed in Paris-blue tweeds
restrained in Mount Auburn's tower.
He stands, his back to me,
seeing mountains, not headstones.

"We must walk those trails one day."

He overlooks paths
twisting past Amy Lowell's grave,
Margaret Fuller's memorial,
Asa Gray's fountain,
footpaths white and pink
with petals from dogwoods,

not my Cambridge streets—
buildings roan, oxblood at midday,
squares teeming with maunderers.

I dream of him, in that tower,
surveying mountains,
paths coiling, deepening,
turning from me,
his right shoulder not as broad as his left,
his left ear larger than his right, turning
so I can kiss the nape of his neck.

An apple floats across my dream.
Golden green. Butter yellow.
Suspended.

THE HEALING WARD

Every day after he stopped touching me
I'd visit the library—
research de Chirico. Once I stole
Antonia White's *Quartet.*

Evenings on Common benches
I'd tell other women and drunks
I was an actress from New York.

No longer riding subway trains,
past back porches—red with geraniums—
past my memory of that night
when he stood at Savin Hill Station—
"I've someone new. But I'll miss our times together."

He'd held an orange foil balloon—
a jack-o'-lantern.
Lamps burned in tenements and walk-ups.
Men, sleeveless, sat on front steps.

I no longer tunnel the Downtown
Crossing, nor imagine sarcophagi
set in dank walls.

I tried to kill myself after he stopped
kissing me. In the ER I panted.
"I don't hear voices."

"A woman can love a man," my roommate
said as she ran her hands down her porcelain thighs.
"A woman can sew curtains, knit lace,
never take too many baths. A woman

can love another woman. But a woman
cannot forgive a man who has no heart."

My de Chirico notes, neatly indexed,
wait at home, on my desk's edge.
I am a book lover and a library.
I am one of Antonia White's "Strangers."

I read my diary aloud. Look over at the woman
sewing in our green community room.
A cup of plastic roses between us.

But I am not a woman who kisses women.

THE ALP AT THE END OF THE STREET

What was it like for you, you ask
lying curled behind me in the hotel bed,
returned to that feeling
of standing close in my dead mother's house
as I showed you her first editions
at the bow window (afternoon pine light through).

We thumbed the past as you spoke of Edwin Land,
recited your work on his dream machine,
how he'd call you early mornings to his house.
Your mutual love of Wallace Stevens
and his fixation with order of words
on the page, his seething. Of Land's dark,
where "one must have a mind of winter..."
you quoted, "and have been cold a long time..."
a land adjacent to your own,
but you called yours Pines,
the sap and the bough
the cones you spray painted the Christmas
you roped yourself to your bed. Out of love?

What was it like for you, you ask
now you've come back to me,
as I sit at the edge of the hotel bed.
You didn't know I saw that you wanted
more than lines and stanzas in somewhat
traditional shape, almost measured,
more than coffee in a sunny chair
in Edwin Land's Brattle Street house—
that you yearned to sit into the night,
if not with him

then alone in a lounge, parked car, run-down
tenement—watch streets from a window
high up, your cigarette smoldering—and hope
for another lover, another fag, another hour in the night.

That day in the curve of the windowseat
returned to the feeling of standing close
(afternoon pine light through)
I made it so you would begin to see
you'd gone to Land out of love, not for a book.

You ask another question, hear another answer,
now that you've come back.

* Edwin Land's dream machine—the entity that eventually was its semi-practical form—
was the short-lived mid-1960's Interactive Lecture System that would let any person access
and ask questions of the best and most articulate expert on a subject.

RUBY-THROATED HUMMINGBIRD

Boxed beneath my bed
lies the ankle-length cloak
I wore three decades ago—
green as a hummingbird's back.

I walked my women's college
in that cloak, brown leather boots
laced up over my calves,
snowflakes filling my book bag.

In the library I found
my French professor's gloves
lying on an empty shelf.
Then the touching began.

Soon I laid my arms around his slender hips,
my cloak catching on the silver buckle
of his black leather belt.

My cloak was our blanket on snowy evenings
in his cold tenement—linoleum tearing,
incense smoldering—but as nights passed,
he turned away.

Now, the man I love—
my aging chemistry professor—
and I do not need a blanket.
He buys rosewater candles
from the body shop,
rubs me down with peppermint.
His beard makes a rash on my thighs.

The taste of his flesh is salty
along his throat, sweet and blossom-soft
between his legs. I hover over him
cloaked in viridescence.

v

GERMAN LESSON, WHEATON COLLEGE 1972

Lighted beneath the hanging lamp,
at one end of the refectory table
a slender sea star reddened.
Miss Willis showed me
sketches of morning glories and tulips,
a branch with its swollen and shriveled sections,
its hairy leaves, identified. Watercolors
of creeks and basins, pastures and evening grosbeaks.
Tracings of da Vinci's study of the human heart.

I sat next to her on the sofa.
She read aloud Werther's July 13, 1771 letter,
and carefully translated, assuming my visit was concern
over German grammar. "I can feel she loves me.
She loves me." She opened Thomas Mann's *Tonio Kruger*,
read aloud first in German, then in her English,
"Art, like love, rests upon sinister foundations."
I understood her. She glanced at the refectory table,
the slender six-armed sea star no longer glowing.

MARGARITAS ON A SATURDAY AFTERNOON IN DECEMBER, DORADO BEACH VIEW CAFÉ

Tubs of red ginger and the macaw in his cage
separated them from the rest of the conferees.
He watched her pick up the cashew bits caught
on her cocktail napkin and put them into her mouth.
He examined her sundress, slate-pigeon,
with bone buttons shaped like marlins.
Some of the buttons had come undone,
but she seemed unaware of that.
Here was a woman who was mostly alone, he thought.

Aloneness. He laughed to himself
as he finished his margarita.
He leaned back in his chair—
he was someone with financial goals,
undergraduate summers of Wall Street training.
She looked to him, head tilted
so her long hair fell to one side.

My face must show how I miss love, she thought
how weary I am of pretending
that I enjoy hanging loose. Last evening
at Cronopios Books, I came across
a man and a woman crouched in an aisle.
He was reading Raymond Carver aloud
and she huddled close against him.
From the next aisle and the next, as I walked away,
I heard him reading, her occasional interruption
and affirmation.

She squeezed a wedge of lime into the last of her margarita.
He moved slightly toward her,
as if only to smell the plumeria tucked in her hair.

4 A.M.

Mist from the harbor sweeps into New Bedford
and she misses the pigeons
in Boston Common, the sparrows
rubbing away grass at the edge of the asphalt walk.

She misses Beacon Hill apartments
where people keep hummingbirds in parlors
and squirrels on leashes, she misses
the Kenmore Square street noise of anger
and beatings and wind grieving. She misses
the Back Bay bookshop, browsing
new fiction, fingering the slimness
of poetry, trespassing among quarterlies,
the plush red carpets, winding
staircase, gold inlay.
It is cool and dark there.

She finds intimacy among the shelves
and brushes against others afflicted
with words, others aroused by the Hopper,
Bosch covers. "Look at me, please."
Confuses book lust for hunger after strangers.

A man in a fedora closes in on her,
his arms filled with books.
She follows him.

From his kitchen window
she sees another kitchen,
across the alley, another linoleum table
with a white bowl of pomegranates.

No lilacs, no oleanders among
the rooftops. The smell of whiteness
festering on brownstones. She folds
into the promise of his touch.

She remembers how she sat on his Sarouk,
how he laid her face down,
slapped her.
It was part of his way. It was hard to leave
his arms when it grew dark, to towel the moistness
between her thighs.

It is 4 a.m. She stares
from long paneled windows
into the moist New Bedford streets.
What she wants most is to be held
down by him. Kissed, kissed, kissed.

WHEN I LEARNED THE NEWS

Swallows swooped through the Coliseum and Forum,
their beaks filled with my breast's blue cells,
and when I awoke in snow, my breast bled from their piercings.

Though I was not a bride, my hands were hennaed.
On pillows embroidered with viburnum and fantail warblers
I lay among a reception of women who balmed—

a pruned breast can grow new flesh. In late January,
I drive past tenements, black and gray train yards
snaking into Boston steel and glass, stop for a tryst

with an artificial life engineer. Afternoon stilled—
his tweeds, my blue dress across the desk, a rented room,
a square of white linen, two sunflowers, some snow.

AFTER SURGERY

I went home and saw that I had died.
The Boston room was bright with lilies.

My Manhattan son and his wife sorted through
books and papers on my desk that had replaced
Hoffmann's *The Sandman* and Le Fanu's *Carmilla,*
books my son and I read together;

evenings of watching him when he was a teen—
booted, long-haired, gig bag slung across his back—
cross Boylston Street from brick buildings,
windows curtained scantily, lighted here and there,
to Daddy's Junky Music Store.

In a gold frame, a photograph of him in a runner's cap
standing in the road that winds by the Coliseum—
the ancient bronzes and laburnum
of its arches and half-columns in the sun.

A nest of a child's wooden blocks on the coffee table—
at eight months he placed a small red block
within a bigger blue block. Hooked
red and green rings over his toy clown.
Built a golden tower of blocks.

I'd peel him apples, their skins coiling like red threads
underneath the paring knife. I'd hand him slice after slice,
eat some myself, the western sun slanting in through the screen door,
the small mounds of apple skins already embers in my lap.

INTERIOR

The lamp is lighted.
The blind drawn.
In that room they are reading
The Discipline of Monogamy.

He in a chair with an antimacassar
opens Lorca's *Three Tragedies.*
She is in a chair by a table,
has chosen Austen, Auster.

Later she will write in her notebook
of his lying beside her
a year of three nights.

She will write of the shine
on her son's legs,
his first birthday skin,
the rose petal stretch
from knees to ankle socks.

She will write of the vagrant
who sat all week leafing
through ample art books
in the Reading Room. Her offer of a meal;
her bed.

They are reading
The Discipline of Monogamy.
She shows him her memories.
He lays aside Lorca, reaches
for more—
wings, nearly dust.

VI

THE MORNING MY SISTER LEFT FOR GOOD

My uncle carried her out in his arms.
The parlor furniture had been polished,

and Fuji mums positioned.
That afternoon, I dressed my doll

in my sister's baby dress.
I danced alone with her in my arms

in the kitchen past the mullion windows
overlooking snowberry and golden glow

the soles of my Mary Janes patting the linoleum.
Daffodil, jonquil, two-layered,

stuffed with Medjool dates, the funeral cake,
baked by my father, cooled on the pantry counter.

THINGS OF SEPTEMBER

Her bedroom door off its hinges.
The bedside table stained with teacup rings,
strewn with pearl hatpins.
The rustle of the white peach tree
against the window screen.
Hello, hello, I whisper.
Grandmother lies still
in her black iron bed.

Summer evenings, I'd creep up to that window,
call, *Hello! Hello!*
I'd see her hats in the cupboard,
its doors left ajar.
The hats—mine to wear, she promised,
when I was grown.

I stand by Grandmother
during all of the calling hours.
Visitors compliment Mother
on her choice of my attire:
velvet hat with gray grosgrain streamers,
coat of dove-colored wool mixed with llama hair.

Before the coffin lid is lowered,
I am lifted to kiss Grandmother,
soft in a blue silk, oil of sweet almond
in her long dark hair.
I touch her hand and turn away.

Back home, I run to Grandmother's cupboard
take out her hats—velvet with veils, feathers
the color of finches and doves—all mine.

FALL RIVER AFTERNOONS, 1955

In Lily's lap, sprigs of Daphne twine
with her sister's remembrance braids.
White stones ring around the pond, home
to one frog her sister named Ichabod Crane.

Lily sits with Grandmother in their garden.
Her doll stands between them.
Phoebes fly in and out of arbor vitae.
Beyond picket fences, neighbor women
pin out lines of colored handkerchiefs—
farewells to dead children—
Lily mistakes them for painted buntings,
her sister's favorites in *The Golden Book Of Birds.*
Tiny pink roses trellis the back wall.
Lily and Grandmother pick dozens of roses,

take them upstairs where Mother lies curled.
Later, Grandmother naps in the chair
by kitchen windows. Room dusks.
Ansonia chimes every quarter hour,
but not even Lily's doll cries.
Lily takes *The Golden Book Of Birds,*
too heavy to hold in her arms, drops it.
Then she spreads it out and kneels over it.

Lily pulls back. Someone's rapping at the front doors.
Lily scribbles on her drawing pad.
Pages gleam with curlicues. Room's dark,
but scribbling makes noise. Room's dark,
but she loops afternoon across the page—
hoses, kids shrieking, *Popsicles!*
called out by roving Candy Man,

tinkling bells sewn to his shirt,
who leaves chocolate rabbits between her front doors.

REMEMBERING MARCH 6, 1955

One step at a time Nana climbed that Sunday morning
I died. You, baby sister, followed behind.
I wore a blue kimono and I'd been waiting for you
by the dresser. But you looked in the mirror instead
of at me, examined your braids, thought them better
than mine. Then Nana gently held your braids
with one hand, reached for mine with the other.

ABSENCE

Were the two of you ever alone?
Were you her sister? Did you ever laugh

after she died, was she your imaginary friend?
Dried peony blossoms—these are from her coffin.

Anything other than that
you were not taught to remember

petals once red, pink, and white
like peonies just before they are deadheaded.

PHOTOGRAPH, NOVEMBER 1951

And my mother, dressed in pink gabardine,
stands in the frosted pasture.
White pines border one edge,
a narrow rutted lane the other.
In the distance is her farmhouse,
the chickens in her coops settling for the night.

A week after this, my mother will marry
the man who reads aloud with her in the evening,
Dostoevsky and Tolstoy,
calls her his Little Russian,
the man who is kneeling before her,
taking her photograph.

My mother smiles. She slips
her hand behind her back to hide
the diamond band she has just been given.
She does not know how her kind of woman
is supposed to act.

Maybe she is missing her little girl's company
and hides her hand-holding hand.
Or she is waiting for the photograph to be taken
so she can run to my father,
draw him up from the land,
place one of his cold hands
between her two slender ones.

GLOVES

The pair folded on her desk
remind her of Monsieur Gendreau's
as he leaned close to her one winter night
in the college library. She was rereading
To The Lighthouse. His were the first,
but others followed—those of the German from Lübeck
demonstrating fishing equipment in New Bedford.
He leaned close to her, but with a different meaning,
for she knew betrayal. From the German,
she progressed to those erasing faux pas
in William Merritt Chase's "A Friendly Call,"
those shielding diaries of adultery on hallway tables
in English novels, concealing aberrations
in Antonia White's *Quartet,* masking the double-bind
in a tryst of her own,
and the last, her father's,
those that covered his fingerless left hand,
the woodchopper's hand she reaches for in her dreams.

SHINE

It happened the hour the nighthawk swooped—
whooping and shrieking—
startled as anyone would be confronting
a hearse on an August midnight in Hixville.
A band of black-coated men and women
hurried up from Trout Brook—
strangers have trespassed these woods for centuries.

In the pine woods outside my bedroom—
the silver hearse—
burned, sooted, choked with scorched silk—
some chrome still intact.

It is the chrome that suggests my mother—
the shine of her back brace—a shine like haiku
that sits between the slant of the desk front and Hamadan,
window glimpsed, ashen mornings.

Makes me think of her '56 Ford Fairlane,
chrome glistening among the bare oaks,
past the mossy sepulchers,
the vandalized tombs—as she drove to my sister's grave. Pinecones,
ice-sheathed, glinted in the wreath, the red
ribbon flared as the sun ice-thawed,
dampening the granite, staining her
gray gloves as my mother traced the epitaph: *I sigh for thee.*

Makes me think of her last days,
her steel walker burnished by fall sunset, as she stood
next to her wing chair, beside the bow window—
mantel run with the length of bittersweet,
a pair of gloves, gray, with cloth-covered buttons—
how her needle-bruised fingers relaxed their grip.

RELIEF

Funeral parlors in brownstones
offer caskets with built-in stereos—relief
from the living, monotone of preacher,
sweet smell of calla lilies, splashes
of rain, trees whirring.
The dead could rock to a favorite dance song,
listen to all of Whitman, study Greek vase painting
through lecture, receive instruction
on the art of the encounter.

Some say this is solace for the living,
consoles the loss of a child half-grown
with Beatrix Potter tapes playing,
a little Frog and Toad voiced
or the loss of a parent who lacked time
to appreciate the hush
of atemporal light in Hopper paintings.

Yet some say these caskets are useless.
Useless as calling an old lover, asking for
one more morning, one more try.
And for a moment you listen
to the white sheet pinned on the line
in the neighbor's back yard—
you consider the sound of it
stretching in the wind
then lifting, and lifting.

A PURE BEAD

I place vases of goldenrod and Queen Anne's lace
and fill the bow window with Sweet Williams.
Then I dust and oil the woodwork
for the feel of it, the motion,
the sight of the room brightening
and I find a moth
gray and long, preserved like Woolf's
on the windowsill.

Without my mother for solace
I imagine the coming spring,
thin sunlight streaking tall pines,
liquescing the ice in the pond.

Today I sit in the parlor chair,
drapes closed against the grove.
I see her walking
through a garden of camellias
somewhere in southern Georgia.
She wears no shroud, talks
of shopping in Fall River
for a Valentine dress
for an eight-year-old me.
I see her, lunching with other crones
in a sunlit café, dressed in blue silk,
a small velvet hat.

I leave my chair
walk into her sunlight,
touch her arm—
"Darling," she murmurs.

Mother,
those evenings I came to your house
to find you waiting,
I looked for your thoughts—
Woolf's moth,
how she wished to turn it
back to front with her pencil,
wanted to right it
for its last act but realized
it was dying. It righted without her.

Those evenings I climbed
your hill, you—a moth
neatly folded, a paper scrap,
waiting for your pencil.

ACKNOWLEDGMENTS

Many thanks to:

—Joan Houlihan, my mentor, for her understanding and inspiration, and with much gratitude for her support for my work.

—Lloyd Schwartz for assuring me more than a dozen years ago that I should be writing poems and for his encouragement over the years.

—Dan Masterson for his encouragement during the past few years.

—John W. Brackett for enabling me to pursue my poetry goals and for his loving support.

—Emerson N. Wong for encouraging me, over the years, to persevere with my writing and for convincing me more than a decade ago that I should write on a computer.

—Stanley Howard, my father, for lifelong encouragement.

—Thelma Portlock Howard (1919-1996), my mother, for her love of literature.

—The following journals in which some of my poems appeared in earlier versions and occasionally in other forms: *2RiverView, Enskyment, Harvard Scriptorium, Oyster Boy Review, Paragraph, Perihelion*

—And with thanks to Ander Monson, Michael Neff, and Del Sol Press.

ALLEGRA WONG lives in Boston, Massachusetts. Her poems have appeared in *Perihelion*, *Passages North*, *Harvard Scriptorium*, *Modern Haiku*, and *Enskyment*—an anthology of previously published poems. Her non-fiction has appeared in *Agni Online*.

She has a B.A. in English from Wheaton College (Norton), and she has done extensive graduate work in English and American language and literature at Harvard University. In the mid-1990s, she was a pioneer in the online teaching field with ReadingWrite, an Internet venture created by her son who is now a multimedia entrepreneur in New York City.

D EL S OL P RESS , based out of Washington, D.C.,
publishes exemplary and edgy fiction, poetry, and
nonfiction (mostly contemporary, with the occasion-
al reprint). Founded in 2002, the press sponsors two
annual competitions:

THE DEL SOL PRESS POETRY PRIZE is a yearly
book length competition with a January deadline for
an unpublished book of poems.

THE ROBERT OLEN BUTLER FICTION PRIZE is
awarded for the best short story, published or unpub-
lished. The deadline is in November of each year.

http://webdelsol.com/DelSolPress

www.ingramcontent.com/pod-product-compliance
Lightning Source LLC
LaVergne TN
LVHW091203080426
835509LV00006B/804